LEAN CREATURES
POEMS

David Coy

ReadersMagnet, LLC

LEAN CREATURES
POEMS

Lean Creatures Poems
Copyright © 2019 by David Coy

Published in the United States of America
ISBN Paperback: 978-1-949981-28-5
ISBN eBook: 978-1-949981-29-2

All rights reserved. No part of this publication may be reproduced, stored in a retrieval system or transmitted in any way by any means, electronic, mechanical, photocopy, recording or otherwise without the prior permission of the author except as provided by USA copyright law.

The opinions expressed by the author are not necessarily those of ReadersMagnet, LLC.

ReadersMagnet, LLC
10620 Treena Street, Suite 230 | San Diego, California, 92131 USA
1.619. 354. 2643 | www.readersmagnet.com

Book design copyright © 2019 by ReadersMagnet, LLC. All rights reserved.
Cover design by Ericka Walker
Interior design by Shemaryl

To my dear sister Sandra who gave me one of her kidneys.

Acknowledgments

Some of these poems have appeared previously in the following magazines:

The Village iDiot: "Deciding to Move"
Slant: A Journal of Poetry: "Homestead on Polecat Bench"
Colorado North Review: "The Legacy"
The Antioch Review: "His Brooding"
Colorado Crossing: "Like Ulysses," "Tamarisk and Painted Lady"

A first edition of this book was published by Church of the Head Press, edited by Jim Jones in 1994 (Pocket Scripture Book 3).

Photos under dedication taken by Canyon Coy and are of a Sculpture created by O.K. Harris.

Contents

PART I: HAIR, BONE & FEATHER

Messengers 12
Lost Lake 13
Confession to Animals 14
Harvesting Pigs 15
Brothers 17
Father's .22 18
Measuring Love 19
Touched by Midas 20
Workers at the Ranger Station 21
The Wednesday Massacre 22

PART II: UNCOMMON GROUND

Homestead On Polecat Bench 24
Among Unmarked Graves of Pioneering Ancestors 28
Encounter 29
The Legacy 30
A Place Worth Coming to 31
The Eucalyptus 33
Neighbor 34
Departure 35
Near Salt River Canyon 36
Tamarisk and Painted Lady 38

PART III: FOR LOVE'S SAKE

His Brooding 40
After Her Affair 41
Black Coffee 42
Breaking the Sound Barrier 43
Like Ulysses 44

Spring Equinox 45
Separation 46
On a Theme by Stephen Spender 47
Puerto Peñasco 48
Jack's Night Song to Lucinda 49
The Same Moon the Same Stars 50
Hurricane Warnings 51
Almost Wilderness 52
Confetti 53
Bona Fide 54
Nebraska 55

PART IV: STRAYS AND CASTAWAYS

Providence 58
In the City of the Homeless 59
Sandra 60
Reaching Beyond Forty 61
The Ones Who Are 62
Ghost Soldiers 63
Following the Service 64
Magpie Man 65
The Impossibility of Standing on Ceremony 66
Somalia, 1992 67

PART I
HAIR, BONE & FEATHER

Messengers

Here he is, relaxed in his lawn chair.
Stars appear as suddenly as static electricity.
He had forgotten about stars.

He holds his glass to his forehead
to deepen his thoughts.

Now there are bats chasing moths,
the big and agile against the small and awkward,
a battle of angles and shadows.
Their conflict is almost silent,
the bat wings snapping faintly like rags in the wind.

He gets up and turns on the pool lights,
not to drive the bats away,
but to draw the moths closer to the water.
Let the bats reveal themselves for what they are,
not just elegant swift loop-makers,
but also lean creatures full of hunger.

On signal they arc over the roof,
fly hundreds of miles
back to their subterranean home.
He wonders how many lost moths
fluttered down like dropped petals.

When he has turned off the light,
one large wing wraps itself around the house
and dips its claw into the pool.

Lost Lake

His uncle and his father
fished from their boat
dead center in Lost Lake,
cast their lines in arcs.
He thought of spiders.
Their catch filled the boat's wide creel.
From the edge he could hear
their voices boom upon the water.

Because the big trout
lolled beneath the surface
and would not take his bait,
he wandered among white birds and frogs,
to a stream's cold mouth
choked with cattail and foxtail,
where floating water lilies
lay open like Eucharist
to the drunken insects.

There he discovered
how hungry the frogs were
for the worm he accidently dangled
as he shifted rod and reel.

Was it wrong for a boy
to fish for frogs,
to let them clamp their mouths
around his hook?

He did it all afternoon
without remorse,
no closer to God,
no further away.

Confession to Animals

Butchering, I removed
the cow's tongue
with my cold blue blade,
peeled back the skin, touched
the bare bone of its jaw
with my fingers, the slippery
grass-stained teeth.

Fishing, I gutted the trout
thrashing on the bank,
sliced the white belly,
pulled loose the eggs and bladder,
getting blood wedged under my nails.

Living, I've done this and more:
reduced live creatures to
blood, skin, bone, hair and feather.

In childhood I left the frog
legless, floating upside down in the pond.
In manhood, brought the buck
sacrificially to its knees.

I put my knife to its throat then,
asking forgiveness from no one.

Harvesting Pigs

Held against their wills,
they scream louder
than terrorized children,
but die in sudden silence
when the gun is fired.

They sink to their knees
as if they've stepped
into soft mud.
They do not kneel.
A memory of odors

fills their nostrils.
When the farmer
cuts their throats,
blood mixes with straw
and manure. After that

they are just raw meat,
although the pink
scrapped and scalded flesh
labored over with long knives
is like our own,

although their roundness
resembles our own.
Then they are what we
want them to be,
fruits of our labor,

quivering loaves
of head cheese, pickled feet,
ham and pork
tender cuts of ham,
succulent slabs of bacon.

Brothers

The way they buck-naked
plunged from the rocks
into the narrow gorge
of surging, muddy water

defied good judgment,
but they knew what to aim for,
knew where the one large boulder
lay submerged, currents

swirling beneath, digging
a hole deep enough
for their daring plummets.
They knew the lore of the river

how everything vaguely loose
gets swept downstream,
how at spring the ice thaws
and the course subtly changes.

But when you are ten, twelve,
thirteen, there is no resisting
a river in hot weather. Summers
they pulled off their clothes

and dived, only in mid-flight
remembering the dump upstream,
with its migratory tin cans
and twisted strands of barbed wire.

Father's .22

The oldest brother,
on his first summer hunting,
seems to have killed
or driven into hiding, everything:
the skunk and quail,
the stray cats littering
in the woodpile,
the porcupine
out at night to chew
rings around the apple tree.
Now the youngest
carries his father's .22
and aims it at sparrows,
aims at the barn—slow animal
crawling toward the haystack—
aims at the sun, thinking
to put it out, to change the world
into one cold Wyoming midnight.

Measuring Love

A child hugs the neck of her horse
which nodding easily lifts her
into the perilous air.
The largeness of what she owns
must overwhelm her.
One hand grabs the loose hair of the mane
while the other clutches
for the star of white skin
bridging the wide tame eyes.
For the horse it is love
not lessened by the coming bridle,
the added weight of the child.

Touched by Midas

We lingered
in the shadow
of a tin roof
and pulled shucks
from ears of corn
delivered by
an old Ford pickup.
The dogs pushed
their noses into
their paws. A few hens
hid in the shrubbery.
In the kitchen
our wives sliced
gleaming teeth
from wooden cobs
to can and freeze.
We admired like lean men
in a fat country
our corn commerce,
work worthy of sweat,
while magpies scolded
from the orchard,
and worms fell
into the soft dust.

Workers at the Ranger Station

Because there was little else to do
we began murdering the mice
who came from the damp grasses
of the meadow to find warmth,
light and music. All summer long
they climbed through the chinks
in the log walls of our cabin. At night
they rattled our cereal boxes,
left twisted tracks across cold skillet grease
built nests of paper in our dresser drawers.

We set out traps along the kitchen counter
in drawers, in cupboard corners.
Then played at playing cards,
pretended not to listen as traps
snapped shut, as backbones were broken.
Alone, we might have shown
them mercy. Collectively, we feigned
indifference. What is one creature
more or less who sticks its nose
into the leftovers uninvited? We tossed
the tiny corpses back into the grasses.

The Wednesday Massacre

Our pup chewed on the faces
of the stuffed animals,
unraveled their fixed expressions
with sharp teeth,
then tore their bodies asunder.
"No, no, bad dog!" we scold.
Bear, Rabbit, Owl
are all dismembered.

Cotton litters the yard,
twisted bits of cloth.
We wonder what to tell the boy
whose body we remember holding
as he held on his lap
these soft creatures.

But it was he
who baited the dog,
who left these sacrifices
one at a time
in flagrant disregard of the past.

PART II
UNCOMMON GROUND

Homestead On Polecat Bench

An adobe shack
defined by the family
living inside four small rooms,
the table pushed up against the stove,
six kids in two bedrooms,
the daughter sleeping beside the youngest son.
So many boys, one lay each night
sideways at the foot of the bed
while the parents slumbered like sentries
in the living room.

Defined by flat, empty land,
whorls of clouds in a flat blue sky,
a few half-dead trees, some loose chickens,
pigs, goats, sheep and cattle
squared off in separate pens,
a cellar covered with a dome of earth.

Driving past
one sees a pair of overalls, the father's,
flying like a flag on the line,
the daughter lifting the baby
onto the seat of the old steam tractor,
the other kids playing hide and seek
behind the rusted Nash
which brought the family here,
then broke down.

And driving further, one sees
the father out in the field on the new tractor,
his face stained by sun,
taking off his cap to wipe his forehead,
exposing his pale scalp.

It is still black and white.
Before the eyes discovered color.
Before psychedelic.
Gray ragweed. Gray juniper.
The chronology is hard to remember–
the year of the lost sheep,
the year of the dead heifer,
the year goats climbed onto the hood of the car
leaving twin indentations
under each cloven hoof.

Perhaps this story, as the family would tell it,
began one morning when they left for church
and the pig chewed through the slats of its pen,
squealed and darted about for the first time
in the open yard. At some point
it found the door of the house
giving way to its curious nose.
Found the trash can under the sink.
Found the canned goods to upset and slobber over.
Found the ten pound sack of flour
and tore it open by shaking it, the way a dog
shakes a slain rabbit or old shoe.

On her return, the mother cursed the God
she had spent all morning praising.

Flour on the floor, in the cracks of linoleum,
on the table, settled in dust upon the window sills,
white powder along the wallpaper, behind the baseboard,
paste on the kitchen utensils
she had placed on the rack to dry after breakfast.

Bad enough the daily invasion of dirt,
but this invasion, this lack of providence,
bad luck which brought her to her knees
cleansing.

Or maybe their story would begin
with the stove's explosion.
The dough risen and pinched into buns,
oiled and arranged on the tray,
the mother leaning over to light
the oven's propane burner. The father would say,
"The gas had been seeping for hours.
Why couldn't she smell it?"
With the explosion, all the pots and pans
piled upon the board shelves
rained down, rattled on the floor,
and the mother rolled to snuff the flames
which leapt from her hair and dress.

Or maybe they would begin by speaking of rain,
of the great downpours
which eroded the adobe walls
and rounded each outside corner,

that softened the earth
so that the house settled into it.
The rain which each spring poured from the eaves,
filled the yard with pools, ran in rivulets,
puddled around the roots of trees and shrubs,
while they huddled under that thin arrangement
of boards covered with tarpaper,
covered with dirt.
How they watched slow drips grow larger
the longer it kept raining.
Cans, glasses, buckets
could not contain it all.

The daughter would add
how the ceiling sagged and caved in
on the night of her prom
as she sat with her date on the couch.

Or perhaps instead of driving past
you stopped. Could be
they wouldn't have much to say
to a stranger. The lean boys
lined up behind the mother and daughter.
The father a bit to one side.
A family gathered beside their driveway.
Not concerned it would seem
with the way things did or did not happen.

Among Unmarked Graves of Pioneering Ancestors

Here, spruce guard the Platte
in a dense row. Twigs
in ice protrude
like scraggly fingers. Dark
shapes skitter like trout.
To see one must walk
quietly along the edge,
not cast a shadow. Where
an arm of stone reaches
through water, I stand alone
to watch the first fall snow
descend--a cover for
the dead. It must have been
this way a century ago,
so cold along the river
travelers watched their breaths
and thought of fire,
live columns of smoke.

Encounter

In a downhill bicycle ride,
he ran over a snake,
a nasty sidewinder.

Too quick to feel
fear or relief,
he focused on balance.

Later he measured his luck–
high legs, low snake,
perfect timing.

He could have fallen
or been struck
could have died later,

but why look backward
through time?
Ahead may be real danger?

The Legacy

We climb down by ladder to examine
a skeleton lying on a ledge in a cavern.

Nothing we find tells us for certain why
when most bones disintegrate these few remain

to show us that a hunter chasing game
fell through a hole (the one we entered)

into an underground lake. That in faint light
he swam ashore to a view of moss-slicked sides.

Nearby we find a turtle cooked in its shell,
his last meal killed and eaten before starvation.

We listen to the sound of sluggish water,
to stalactites dripping, two centuries too late.

When bats fly past us toward some dark interior,
We move with caution back to where we started.

A Place Worth Coming to

The pickup bounces
barely stirring dust.
Our driver, a neighbor
in his eightieth year,
turns to tell tales,
not watching the tracks
zag through sparse wild grass.

We ride gripping our seats
and sliding together, listen
to his stories, discolored
as sun-tinted glass (flasks
thrown on the prairie
by prospectors or cattlemen).
He embellishes on the past.

Says in 1933
as a ranch hand riding fences
he passed a circle of bluffs
beside a fork in the river...
saw a village of teepees,
children running naked.

Bare breasted women leaning
over pots. Blackfoot or Arapaho?
He did not know, but marked
the spot by memory--
a place he would come back to.

And sure enough we find
on the last turn before dusk
where the road peters out,
teepee stones scattered among
dry cow dung. In failing light
we find a talisman.

We claim it as a place worth coming to,
but he is disappointed,
on the way back, silent.

The Eucalyptus

Its leaves catch light
like a thousand
fluttering wind chimes.
Here a teenager hung herself
after drinking
from a bottle of Johnny Walker.
She was thinking,
"Why live without love?"
(Her boyfriend gone,
victim in a car wreck.)
Unless you wait for new love
there is no good answer.
"Tomorrow or the next day,"
says the local paper,
"this tree will be cut,
to erase this tragic case
from the public's memory."
What would she say?
She chose this place
of living wood?

Neighbor

His house is in the hollow
on the corner that turns so sharply
you never get a good look at it.
His cows with their black, sleek bodies
and white faces are more familiar.
This man with his gun and black lab,
with his sharp whistle that brings the dog running.
is always moving at a distance, walking,
his car never driven it seems,
his children all grown and gone elsewhere.
Smoke comes from the chimney, alright.
One day he'll show up
on your porch, frantic and confused,
and you'll wish you had never met him.

Departure

We damned the trailer
for its flimsy hitch, the car
for its bald tires and dirty oil.
We wept good-bye to friends,

then packed our coffee cups.
We sorted, boxed then carted
all: dressers, nightgowns, dolls,
the skeleton of a gar,

the kid's big box of toys,
a bronze bust of e e cummings,
a guitar, her antique clothes,
twelve scarves with matching hats.

All day the stairs groaned
under our heavy loads.
The air conditioner,
kicked off and on.

We were fools to cram it
into one domestic package.
The walls we left
breathed new life, a welcome.

Near Salt River Canyon

The train rides
above the fragile town
of warped wood houses
above enduring hills
of cactus and creosote,

runs on rails
suspended on poles
above a ravine
laced green
from slag water.

Another summer
comes simmering
to its close. Scorched
trees line the streets
like derelicts.

The oldest house
sits close to ruin.
Stray dogs sleep
in its shadows.
Its thin roof in wind

rasps out a whisper.
I would not belong here
even if I stopped
and dug with hands
into the soil,

for those who stayed
lie in graves
half covered with rocks
and riddled with holes
of ground squirrels.

Tamarisk and Painted Lady

When tamarisk bloom
in the land of saguaro
and slender, blood-tipped ocotillo,
the desert turns blue-green and gray like haze,
so sky and hills and tamarisk
drift dreamlike in the traveler's eye.

And where the tamarisk thrive
there is promise of water,
the moist blessing of earth,
though at a distance
the small-leaved petals seem parched
and sunburnt.

They camouflage a willowy greenness
where one can discover
as if breaking a pomegranate open
the painted lady,
half-moth, half-butterfly,
her wings folded together,
the undersides bright orange
with brownish swirls,
the top wing colors gray.

Among the strokes of blurred
and muted colors
lucky the traveler who sees
a dozen painted ladies fly
from the inner sanctum
of one tamarisk.

PART III
FOR LOVE'S SAKE

His Brooding

I watch fist-sized shadows
flying under birds

skimming the dappled ground—
leaves, half light, half dark web.

I lean on my own shadow,
become the death I always was.

Behind the sun, a pitch black orb
burns with such intensity

blossoms retract, green stems
dry into sticks. For love's sake

I think of a woman laughing
as she sorts and hangs bright socks,

green, red, yellow, blue
in a yard where stones light up.

After Her Affair

All afternoon she stays in the pool
her shoulders turning red,
the rest of her body pale.

She tries to wash away all guilt.

She watchs a wasp
stuck to the surface,
its wings a crucifix,
try to pull loose and fly.

Soon it will be mere flotsam.

Her body dangles at odd angles,
a monotonous buoyancy.
Her mouth breaths just inches
above water.

He can not share
her rue, her pity.

Black Coffee

Today my anger is black coffee.
I have forced sleep from my eyes
by pouring bitterness down my throat
because someone has forgotten to buy sugar.
My wife has wisely crawled under running water
where my voice cannot travel.
She has hung her black nightgown
like a truce flag on the bathroom doorknob.
But I refuse to make peace.
I'll nurture this life without sweetness,
grow moody and impatient,
hope wanting makes getting
that much better.

Breaking the Sound Barrier

From an afternoon swim,
we drove with loud music
trailing behind our car,

left the farmer
on his tractor in its wake.
The heat came through

our open windows
over our damp bodies.
Our nakedness stuck

to the vinyl upholstery.
In my mind, I kept
the long gorgeous curve

of your body.
In a grove of oaks
we parked and made love

with the radio still blaring.
Later, on my patio, in darkness
we turned off the radio

and listened to the sounds
our music
had silenced.

Like Ulysses

On my return
I listen for a while
to boats rasp
against their moorings,
to a social entanglement
of noisy sea gulls.
There is the faint,
phlegmatic cough
of an old sailor come
to cock an eye
at the blazing horizon.
Waves strike
against the rocks
like a desire.
Before I go to
the woman I love,
I will open my shirt
like a sail,
hold up both arms and
let the damp sea air
inhabit me.

Spring Equinox

We cover our naked bodies
and grow inward.

Our limbs stretch to find comfort.
They wrap up in each other.

We curl and uncurl in darkness.
We let go of concern,

let our muscles release from effort,
let the mind disconnect from its source.

Like curved sprouts we sleep under open windows
and wait for new light to reach us.

Separation

Fear poses questions.
Anger makes declarations.
So, he does not ask
or say anything.
Instead, he listens
to his sandals slap
on the sidewalk.
Two lovers pass
in a convertible--
their laughter lingers
even after the car
has turned the corner.

If he had the courage
he would keep walking
the two miles to where
his wife is staying.
He would discard fear
and put on a feeling
impervious to language
since love is an imperative.

On a Theme by Stephen Spender

Because you did not love enough
and afterwards loved too much,
you deserve the hurt, to live
through a time when leaves
are hearts of stone, when green
is unbearable. You deserve
the world as ghost, the invisibility.

Because you lacked the confidence
to choose, you have yourself
to blame. You may as well
pull down the blinds, hop into bed
and read a book whose words
are ash and meaningless.

Read a poet who compares
his love to spring in the face
of certain change: to summer,
fall, winter and death.
You built the cross, go crucify
yourself. Shame. Double shame.

Puerto Peñasco

They walked
The gleaming edge
Where land met ocean,
Two long-term lovers.
This was as close
As they would ever come
To eternity: water,
Sand and night sky
Blending together,
Myriad white shells,
Exquisite spiraled cones,
Empty gnarled chambers.
The bodies once alive inside
Were dead and dissolved.
Holding each other,
They climbed the coarse
Volcanic rocks
Back to their car,
Their bare feet
Bruised and bleeding.

Jack's Night Song to Lucinda

I still find solace
standing under the stars
which do not actually
wrap around us

but burn
at a cold distance.

I walk under them
to the nearest bar,
put a coin in the jukebox,

join conversation,
drink alcohol,
to ease the thought:
you would not marry me.

My loss is small,
kindling spent
to feed a greater fire,
unlike a failure of desire

The Same Moon
the Same Stars

A man leaves the bus,
enters a strange town,
the one on a familiar address. He watches
the touchstone faces behind the windows
of the Greyhound dissolve
into near darkness.

Across town, the woman
he travels to see
enters her balcony for a breath
of night air. She remembers
his letter, that he is coming

and shivers. Does she really
want him? She stares
at the moon, at its flat
circular surface
the color of Chablis.

For him, the moon resembles
the parched circle
where the water hose has lain
curled too long.
For both, it is a mirror
without the image of one's face.

Hurricane Warnings

If the light stays on,
he'll read,
but if she gets up
and clicks it off,
they'll roll over,
face each other
in darkness, kiss,
make love slowly.
As the river swells
against its banks,
they will imagine
a flood large enough

to send small
unhappy creatures
scrambling for dry
dangerous places.

Almost Wilderness

Camping with his wife, he awakens
after the fire has burned down to a few red embers.

Overhead, a circle of stars
seems to sway with the trees in the wind.

Cicadas shrill to each other
their articulate cries of courtship.

A creature wades slowly in the river.
He hears its tongue lap water.

They are alone by choice
their car in a distant campground.

He adjusts his body to fit the contours of her body.
The two of them wrapped in a cocoon of cotton and nylon.

Confetti

A man feeds
chopped up newspaper
into the fireplace
after New Year's Eve.

His wife returns
when the party is long over
claiming to have stepped out
for olives.

Somehow they were forgotten.

The words mid-life,
Cadillac, pantyhose,
float in snowflakes
behind the sofa.

One phrase from Ann Landers
lodges in the carpet, underfoot:
...stark naked opened
the door to the mailman.

Words fly
like sparks and paper ash.

Soon he is packing.

His wife crops his image
from their wedding picture

Bona Fide

My Love is bona fide coo coo,
made of electricity and adrenaline—
not just afraid of spiders, but able
to see them dismantling her furniture.

She loves me for my sanity,
the way I rescue her from fantasy,
keeping the truth soft for the long drop.

When the car she drives takes
a sharp turn into the rails
on the steepest incline, and she barely stops
at the precipice, my whispered encouragement
pries her fingers from the wheel.

Then it is I driving her home,
fear like a trailer slipping from its hitch.

Nebraska

What strange creatures grow up in Nebraska!
Man-avoiding rabbits. Owls who sit on dead limbs,
mouse tails hanging out of their beaks.
Deer corn-high and mute—playing hide and seek
in uncut grass. Play-dead possums and quarreling
squirrels. In Nebraska, women are wild
as the un-hatched moon. They move through cycles.
Harvest woman becoming blue woman. Corn woman
becoming oak woman. Whiskey woman becoming
potato peel woman. It's crazy as gnats flying
up your nose. It's goofy as crawling under a bush
of blackberries and reaching up to pluck a few.
No man in his right mind enters Nebraska
without his rifle. No single man enters
without wearing a ring on one of his fingers.
On any day Jehovah can grow horns and offer you
crushed grapes in a golden chalice.

PART IV
STRAYS AND CASTAWAYS

Providence

Gray light
has emptied the trees
of their color—
but he stands

in the snow
with naked feet,
where the last leaves
and pods of fall fell—

a sparrow
in winter twilight
digging crusted snow.
Once fat as Friar Tuck,

he's now hungry and down
on his luck
with bare beak
chipping away.

In the City of the Homeless

A sick pigeon
assaulted by others
huddled on the ledge
of the Sir Francis Drake Hotel.

One eye was gone
and numerous feathers.

He peered down suicidally
three dizzying stories
at me waiting for a bus.

Though I am no hero, I played
at being a fireman:
I spread my coat between my arms
to catch him.

Of course, he did not jump.

The others
moved in beside him, pecked
until he staggered, fell.

I thought I had him.

What I had,
I left wrapped in my coat
upon the sidewalk.

Sandra

The day she entered the hospital
I spilled bleach
on the kitchen floor,
on the gray concrete,
now blotched with whiteness.
She was in a bed on wheels
in sheets so clean and starched,
by comparison her skin was yellow.
On my knees I wanted another chance,
wanted the bleach to re-enter the bottle
and the stain to shrink into nothing.
I wanted the white cells in her blood
to kill the mutineers
on board to steal the treasure
of her life. I was rubbing the spot
making things worse –
hoping fresh bone marrow
could rejuvenate her,
knowing some things you just have
to accept, but not immediately,
certainly, and not all things.

Reaching Beyond Forty

A wasp caught between window and screen
has died from heat and exhaustion,
but my life has opened up.

The circles of loss and grief
have been pushed away
by the smaller circle of daily pleasures.

My neighbor, a septuagenarian widow,
sweeps her sidewalk each evening
with a broom worn down several inches,

unconcerned that the dust of autos undoes
her work, that a nearby cinder block factory
sends out ashes and more ashes.

The Ones Who Are

The ones loved before seen
have perfect innocence.
A place has been created
to shelter their nakedness.
Their mirrors have no dust.
They are hushed asleep
to orchestral music.
Love seems easy to them.

Others are blemished
with the first touch.
Their bruises spread
like the over ripeness in fruit.
They are prisoners in their rooms.
They rock themselves to sleep
with anger. Love swells
like a blister under their tongues,
and they cannot speak
their desires without pain.

Ghost Soldiers

An army marches Halloween night
through the confederate cemetery
on a hill near Fayetteville. They walk
in gunsmoke fog, each soldier
pale and cold as a slaughtered hog.
Some guns slung over the shoulder,
some loosely, hanging down,
they stumble in shambles
toward remembered battle ground,
toward the sad rock-hard conclusion
of death at Wilson Creek.
If you should witness them,
it would be wise to salute. They could
be your southern kin. They could be
whom you might have been. Don't look
at their eyes. You'll see their fate,
and feel an infinite sadness
born of hate.

Following the Service

"Death shall have no dominion"
                                      –*Dylan Thomas*

It was time to be serious
   to suffer
but I sat upon a stump
in the open field
and welcomed the happy music
of a mockingbird and a cardinal
and the sight of flowers
randomly together—
the blond field strewn with white daisies,
the sun lucidly yellow.
I was breathing without fear
not breathing would be fatal,
not diminished
by a friend's sad claim
   poets are too fragile
   to live in the real world
or by the preacher's sermon—
   Suicides Don't Get into Heaven.
Not diminished.

Magpie Man

I remember a man
post-depression era
who colored his graying hair
with shoe polish,
who slicked it back
and buttoned the top button of his shirt
and smiled too damn earnestly,
who had memorized phrases,
"Doesn't that just put the wind
back into your sails.
Who carried a big leather valise
stuffed with papers,
who mended the worn soles
of his shoes by slipping cardboard
under his feet,
who came at dinner time.
to sell us encyclopedias
and begged with his eyes
to be invited to stay,
who could not hide his hunger
or his sorrow,
who stood beside his car
as the sun began to sink
in the west and pulled.
a small flask of whiskey
from an inside pocket,
and in an unguarded moment
tilted his head upwards
and swallowed.

The Impossibility of Standing on Ceremony

One steps into ceremony
as one steps into a stream,
never in the same place twice.
Sometimes it is turkey and pumpkin,
sometimes wafers and wine.
Sometimes the ring is slipped onto the finger.
Sometimes slipped off, put into a drawer.

One looks from the bus window
at a blur of houses
in the old neighborhood,
coming or going.

According to ceremony,
it's either hugs,
handshakes, kisses or waves.
Fingers press on window glass
or rest in the lap.

It boils down to this,
a breath like any other breath,
a day like any other day,
the sun still young and predictable.

Somalia, 1992

The earth yields little greenery
along miles of hard grayness.
Small, mangy birds skitter in suspicion
toward trees stripped of leaves and bark.
Even insects are wily
and infrequent.

In this place
the newborn's cry for milk
cannot be easily answered.
Everyone alive or dead
is a parchment and scroll
even the blind could read.

Numbness, delirium
are blessings
when each day
the righteous dead are planted
and still nothing succulent grows.

www.ingramcontent.com/pod-product-compliance
Lightning Source LLC
LaVergne TN
LVHW040200080526
838202LV00042B/3257